Harold

A Wise but Unpretentious

Man

Harold

Harold was not an extraordinary person, except perhaps in living a longer life than most. Like all of us he was a victim of circumstances, a man of his era, and a product of a less than perfect education system. Harold was keenly interested in the world around him and he cared about humanity. He knew that some struggles are worthwhile and that some are not, somethings are worth a battle, some are not.

Logically it would seem that the longer we live the more stories of our lives we have to tell. But Harold's stories did not increase greatly in number over the years. Being a man not given to speaking, to use his own phrase, 'waffle and twaddle', to fill gaps in conversation, his stories were of those experiences that exerted the most influence on him, in their various ways, over the 98 years of his life.

Harold was not an extraordinary person, but he was a wise, unpretentious man who lived a long life and left the world no worse for his having been here. Here are some of the stories from his life.

The Story of the Cow and the Stile

Of course we don't know why it was that Harold took the particular route that he did, or even what business took him out across the fields that dark night. We know only that it was dark, it may even not have strictly speaking been night-time. In the countryside, away from street lights and other artificial illuminations of nature's darkness, 4pm can be dark, while 10pm can be light. If dark is night then night is an ever-changing thing. In mediaeval times, and before, night was understood to precede day whereas now day is thought to precede night. But in our collective consciousness do we still hold the memory that night precedes day. We talk of Christmas Eve, the eve of Christmas Day, its coming. Of course nowadays anytime on December 24th is deemed to be Christmas Eve, whereas previously the eve of Christmas began at nightfall and marked the beginning of the day when the Christian church celebrates a mass for the assumed birth of Christ. Overcome with a desire to order the lives of all, to ensure that everyone moves to the same rhythm and that the rhythms remain unchanged through the year, we have sought to regulate time itself. With our fixed hours for work, for study, for leisure we have created days and nights that are of equal length throughout the year, ignoring the true rhythms of nature.

Nature does not decree that we should have days and nights of regular lengths but rather that days and nights should differ quite wildly in length in this corner of the northern hemisphere. In the summer when there is food to harvest and store, nature has given us more daylight and less dark. It's like she is saying yes, I know there is much to do now but see there is also light in which to do it. In the winter, when many of our trees, plants and animals need colder weather to allow them to die back or sleep, nature compensates us with more darkness to aid our own rest.

So maybe, when Harold took that particular route, it was night in the old meaning and not the new. Perhaps we might assume it was 6pm, was he returning from the nearby home of his paternal grandparents? 'That was home from home', he would say in later years – much later years for we now know that he would live, against all his expectations, and the expectations of many others, to a very old age.

There are three things we know: that Harold was not yet an adult but beyond being a child (although that was a different age when

5

children were able to attain independence at their own pace, by the early years of the 21st century children of 8, 9 and 10 years or more are seen being taken by the hand by their fearful parents all the way to the school door, from the point at which their parent has squeezed into an inadequate parking space, in the car that creates the very hazards that they fear for their child.)

The second thing which we know is that there was darkness, when the tale is told in later years, to children, grandchildren and great-grandchildren, it is clear that the dark is significant and that this is real darkness, countryside darkness, maybe it is a night in the dark phase of the moon's cycle or maybe it is before the moon has risen. But the darkness is nothing to fear, Harold was not fearful to be out alone in the dark, he had done this many times and the dark was not more to be feared than the light. It just required a different use of senses, knowledge and perception. If he heard the tawny owl calling did he know instinctively which direction it came from? As he ran across this field did he know how long he must run for before reaching the style? Probably he did for the third thing we know is that this was a familiar route to him. We know this because he told it in his story, 'been that way hundreds of times', 'I knew how big the style was', and, recalling the sure footedness and confidence of the young, 'no problem climbing the style even though it was dark, just did I what I always did, stood on the top and jumped off the other side'.

But we don't know why he was making that journey, taking that walk. Almost certainly we don't know this because it has no bearing on the tale being told. He was never one for elaborating unnecessarily, he didn't need to be. We don't know at what point in the year the story took place but it wouldn't be midsummer, nor indeed mid-winter unless a very mild winter, because the cows were still in the fields. Did he run because the weather was cold? Or wet? Did he run because he was late, or did he run just for the pleasure of running in the dark, in the wind – children, released from the constraining hands of adults, love to run in wild and windy weather, that's a massive sensory experience for them. But put yourself in his shoes, or rather his boots because this was the days when everyone who could afford to wore strong leather boots that kept their feet warm and dry, helping to make them unafraid to be out in inclement weather. Imagine yourself in the experience, running through the dark, anticipating the stile between the two fields, reaching the stile just when your calculations told you that you would, reaching for the top with your hands and pulling as your feet instinctively found the step, balancing momentarily on the top ready for your flying leap into the next field. And leap, feel the wind rushing past you, the exhilaration of the brief moment when you are suspended in the air, a moment that seems to last and last, although in reality only a second or two long, and then – chaos – you've landed on a cow, sleeping in the lee of the gate, a now terrified cow, staggering to its feet as you fall beside it, how close did you come to being trampled, to serious injury, to death, how fragile and easily damaged our lives can be? But this was not Harold's moment for injury or death, he lived on to tell the tale many times.

Telstar

Telstar, a space age instrumental recorded by The Tornadoes in 1962, born of the technical ingenuity, the willingness of the innovative and now legendary music producer, Joe Meek, to have a go, to experiment, to be prepared to fail, and to try again. Harold knew that what mattered was not whether he, himself, liked the music but whether he understood that without such experimentation, without innovative people prepared to fail, prepared to try again when they did fail, prepared to run with their ideas no matter how alien to the times, we would all be the poorer. All through our lives we each meet a different set of challenges, experiences, pleasures and displeasures, from all of these comes understanding of the world and people around us. Taking the opportunities that our lives present our individual knowledge store equips us to make use of the good, and the not so good, that we encounter as we make our way through life. There is no one right way to live, to love or to show that we care, we are all novices in this game of life. We experiment and try things out as we go along, sometimes we fail, sometimes we try again, and sometimes we don't. Sometimes we do what is best for others, sometimes we don't. Sometimes we know if we have acted

for the best and sometimes we don't know.

Jam

Jam, did Harold's mother make jam? Probably she did. In those post war days of his childhood, in the 1920's, who could afford to let a glut of plums or strawberries go to waste when a couple of hours work would preserve them for the winter? Did Harold help his mother, did he hull the strawberries, pick the raspberries, and carry home baskets of plums from generous neighbours? For if neighbours had a plum tree and a fine crop of plums, all ripe at the same time and all with the same short lifespan, then they needed to distribute their plums rapidly. Maybe they had, also, a desire not to waste valuable food in those impoverished times. Were they most glad for having homed their plums, for having helped their neighbour, or for the sense of satisfaction they felt knowing that they would be seen as kind and generous? Or maybe they were mindful of what they might, one day receive in return when their neighbours had cause to remember this generosity.

And what about the blackcurrants? Picking those tiny berries off the stalks was surely a labour of love performed only by those who unreservedly loved either the blackcurrant jam or the jam maker, or possibly those compelled by the jam maker to help – for those were the days when children were still believed able to carry out tasks to assist the running of the household – yes even tedious or mundane tasks, not for themselves but for their family's welfare.

In later years Harold rarely ate jam, being instead dedicated to marmalade consumption right until the end of his life, but he knew something of jam and what it has become. He knew that strawberries were a luxury fruit, a short, unpredictable, growing season kept the price high. A short lifespan once picked meant strawberries were picked, marketed, bought and eaten in one day – a top quality luxury, available for a short time each summer to anyone who could grow them or afford to buy them. For most of his adult years Harold would grow a few strawberry plants. Was that because instinctively he wanted to give his children a taste of strawberries as a real luxury? How he bemoaned the mass production of tasteless strawberries in the last years of his life. After all, it's not a luxury or a treat if it's available every day and how narrow do our lives become without the knowing of luxuries and treats. When these things were more generally appreciated the greengrocers knew better than to try and sell day old strawberries for eating, these were sold half price and clearly labelled 'jam strawberries'.

Strawberry jam – a luxury – the most expensive jam in the grocers' shops, reserved perhaps for Sunday tea on fresh scones. But plums, they arrive in huge numbers, a tree full, an orchard full, lots of orchards full ready for the making of that everyday standby, inexpensive to make and inexpensive to buy – plum jam. The 1920's larder might contain a dozen jars of plum jam to one jar of strawberry jam. Even when money was very short only the very poorest could not afford a jar of plum jam to add to plain bread or to put in suet puddings to fill up hungry children.

And then all that changed because supermarkets arrived. Of course in the early days of supermarkets there were no automated tills telling the checkout staff the price of goods. Checkout staff needed to remember the price of all the goods sold. Trial and error, and probably a number of irate customers, showed that checkout operators could mostly remember 200 prices, and so simplified pricing was introduced. All jams the same price – well who would buy plum jam when they could have strawberry jam for the same price? So what choice did the farmers have, once in the grip of the demands of the supermarkets, but to rip out their now worthless plum orchards and look to ways of producing enough strawberries to meet this new demand? Of course if we want the plum orchards back there's an even bigger problem because many of them, like the one behind the house Harold lived in when his children were young, have been built on.

But plum jam is making a comeback – now an 'artisan' jam, a luxury food, available at a premium price.

Driving

Sometimes in life making the most of the situation and taking the opportunities offered may be the best options available because sometimes, in every life, there are times when choice and free will are not options. Whatever freedom we may aspire to, and freedom means different things to different people, may simply not be available.

Harold's own choice would never have been to join the armed forces but that's where he found himself in 1941, while those who made the decision to send him to war sat safe and more comfortable, directing the destinies of others from their offices. Safe, but not getting Harold's respect. Because, whatever the situation, real respect is earned, not a right of position or power. Harold liked to tell the story of the newly appointed, fresh from university, railway station manager he encountered in later years. This man could not comprehend why the staff he supposedly commanded had so little respect for him that they sometimes declined to complete basic tasks such as sweeping the station platform. He, who had never known a real days physical work, never needed to get his hands dirty, and yet they showed so much respect for his predecessor, a man who had once been one of them and had worked his way up the ladder to achieve his management position. When this predecessor had asked them they swept the platform, because they knew that he too had swept the platform, in rain, in snow, in sun, on days when he felt good, and on days when he really needed to be elsewhere. And they knew that, if circumstances required it, he would again sweep the platform with them. Good leaders are made but they aren't made in colleges and universities.

Another, briefer story Harold liked to tell, a passing moment observed in the lives of others. Walking through a Woolworth's store, passing the confectionary counter where loose sweets were weighed into bags by a young lady store assistant. A young man passing by observed stray sweets fallen to the floor, his badge declaring him to be 'trainee manager', hands behind his back, wearing a suit, surrounded by an arrogant air of his own self-importance, likely to be fresh out of education on a management training scheme. Officiously informing the young lady store assistant, 'these sweets need picking up'. Can he not see the queue of customers she is serving? But this day, a lesson for him, because this day he is not walking alone through the store but with a much older manager, who probably attained his position before the days of graduate management training schemes, he probably gained his position through years of experience. He asks the young man what the problem is, the young man says, 'I've asked her to pick up the sweets from the floor and she hasn't done it'. 'Bend your back boy', comes the prompt response, 'bend your back'. Yes Harold loved that story.

But back to making the most of opportunities. In the armed forces Harold found himself tied to a military life until the powers that be were willing to release him, 'thank you for doing your duty, we're so glad you're still alive, here's a reference so that you can go and find a job'. *'A man in whom the highest trust can be placed. Intelligent. Highly recommended for any confidential work.'* What happened to those with far less favourable references when the war machine finally spat them out to find their own way in the world?

Not many of Harold's stories were about his military years but a couple, one the small victory of another observed, and the second a skill learnt, reflect experiences from those military years that influenced Harold.

It is often the case that people are more comfortable in any situation if they know that there is someone else who is worse off than them, lower down the scale than them, less skilled than them, just as with the managers in those other stories told. Early days conscripted into the army, a mass of nervous young men, isolated from family and often from friends, needing to make new bonds, new friendships, desperate not to be bottom of the heap. The less confident look immediately for someone to target. And one young man, big muscular, with already several years labouring work behind him and still not risen from the bottom of the heap at his workplace, decides this won't happen to him again, not here in the army. He quickly identifies his target, the tall, very slim, slightly effeminate young man and starts an argument. He wants a fight, he needs to show his strength, he needs everyone to know he isn't going to be bottom of the heap. As he lunges towards the tall, slim young man, the tall, slim young man, drawing on the years of training he has undertaken in his own workplace, picks up the bigger, muscular man and throws him lightly across the room. Confident that he will attract no more negative attention he has no need to take the fight further, only when pressed by others does he divulge that his previous training and work required immense physical strength, for he is a ballet dancer.

And the skill Harold learnt, the opportunity taken? Harold learnt to drive. Of course these days so many people learn to drive but in Harold's youth this was not the case, there were only around 2.5 million cars in the country, now there are over 38 million. Harold always remembered who taught him to drive and how well he was taught. Eight hours a day, six days a week for several weeks that was his initial training. Driving every vehicle available, sometimes with a sheet stretched over all the controls, training drivers to keep their eyes on the road and to instinctively know where the controls were. Driving a vehicle with no brakes, training in how to stop a vehicle if the brakes failed, even at speed. So there we are, he didn't want to be in the army but he came out of the army a very good driver.

The Pig Sty

When you have a birthday in January and you live in northern latitudes there are certainties surrounding your birthday which you can always rely on. Chief of these is that your birthday will be cold and that daylight hours will be short.

In the years leading up to 1941, what dreams or expectations did Harold have for his 21st birthday which would fall in January of that year? Those were days when 21 was the age of majority, the age of enfranchisement, a birthday bringing with it the right to vote. The right to elect the government that would rule lives and put in place policies which, just as today, might almost randomly assign people as winners or losers in the game of life. This enfranchisement came to Harold a full seven years after the start of his working life. For his mother a generation before him who, as a woman, was not given the right to vote until she was 30 years of age, this enfranchisement was her reward for 18 years of work, starting in the Lancashire mills at the age of twelve. Of course, Harold would tell us in later years, the 'education' provided for the children of working class families such as his mother's at the end of the 19th century was education in name only. To leave school at 12 one had only to pass the necessary school leaving test, a test which required little more than the ability to write one's own name.

The real purpose of this 'education' was not to open opportunities, not to inspire ideas and creativity, or lead children to expect more from life, a greater slice of the pie. No, its main purpose was to ensure that these children could function at the level required of them to keep the wheels of industry turning – to make Britain great. How far, as a society in the 21st century, have we truly progressed from such a position? Perhaps the more things change the more they remain the same.

But we must not forget also the trials endured by more affluent children. In their middle and upper class worlds at that time the pursuit of knowledge was obligatory. Positions in society needed to be maintained, for fear of descending to the level of the masses. How many of those children spent their school days wishing they did not have to engage with the education that many working class children thirsted for?

But we digress and so back to Harold's story. One day in January 1941 Harold woke to the realisation that this day was his 21st birthday. He also woke to the realisation that the occasion would not be marked, except in his own mind and probably also in the minds of those who loved him and wished him home safe. On that day in January 1941 he woke up to yet another day in army uniform, with the daylight hours and possibly some of the dark, spent marching through snow and ice. We think he was in Scotland but we don't know why, in ill-fitting boots because the army did not care too much if its soldiers had ill-fitting boots – possibly because they weren't expected to last too long – the soldiers not the boots. Undoubtedly many more army boots than soldiers survived what would later become known as the Second World War. 'That was my 21st birthday', Harold would say in later years, that was the day when he became entitled to vote to elect the government of his country.

Throughout his long life he never missed a vote for he knew that others had fought and died for the right to vote. This battle they had chosen to fight.

On this march, in the snowy depths of a Scottish winter, or possibly on a different snowy march, this time in Belgium, it doesn't really matter which, the incident of the pig sty occurred. Europe was at war and everywhere in turmoil, armies marched from this place to that place, exhausted young men just doing what they were told to do because, well maybe because they thought doing so would give them the best chance of getting home alive, possibly even in one piece. Actually, although this doesn't usually get much of a mention, there were upwards of 100,000 deserters from the British army roaming around Europe during this war *('The Deserters: A Hidden History of World war II', by Charles Glass)*. Anyway, the ones that stuck it out - for whatever reason – spent a lot of time marching around with not always, probably not often, a cosy billet at the end of the day. On this march the day ended at a farm, an early 1940's farm, no doubt similar to the one where Harold had spent some of his youth. Water from a well, pigs to turn waste into food, a farm house, probably kept warm with a wood fire, at least in the big kitchen – the heart of the home. The soldiers didn't know the fire and the kitchen of course because they were left to make what arrangements for their night's accommodation that they could in the farm yard. No doubt the officers enjoyed the more congenial, and infinitely warmer, accommodation afforded by the farm house, which, if nothing else, did not have snow falling in it. Well the things we learn through life can come in useful at the strangest times, how could he have known, in his early days on a farm, called on to clean out the pigsty, that he would learn something which would prove very useful on this bleak, and freezing, winter's night?

Someone identified that the pig sty would make a better shelter than the open yard. We don't know if it was him or someone else who chased the pig – or maybe there was more than one pig – out of the pig sty. What we do know is that the city bred soldiers refused to sleep where any pigs had been sleeping while he and another country bred young lad, welcomed this spot, filled with clean dry bedding as well as the warmth left by the pigs, for they knew that pigs are clean animals, they keep their sleeping quarters clean, they don't sleep in their own dirt. That was on the other side of the sty waiting to welcome the city bred soldiers to a smelly night.

Government Money or a Citizen's Wage?

What do we, as a society, benefit from creating an underclass? Surely this financially costs more, through demands on health services, through crime and its consequences both to the victim and the perpetrator, as well as creating a class of people who can only contribute positively to the wider society through monumental effort and sacrifice on their own part. Surely when the effort outweighs any benefits they must ask themselves, why should I bother? When a person, although working full-time on the minimum wage, is unable to pay their rent, council tax, utility bills and afford a healthy diet, with some money to spare for leisure activities that protect mental and physical health, surely then, we as a society have gone wrong. This happened in the 1920's and 1930's, it's happening again almost a century later.

But suddenly, when war was declared in 1939, the government found money to fund the conflict despite having told the unemployed that their lives of extreme poverty and sometimes destitution could not be alleviated by higher unemployment pay throughout the years now known as 'the great depression'. The sacrifices that they had unwillingly made during these years, inadequate living conditions and inadequate health care, children sick or dead as a result of inadequate nutrition. The often devastating effects on physical and mental health as families found themselves unable to provide for their children, their elderly and their vulnerable adults, years spent waiting for things to improve, these sacrifices counted for nothing they failed to prompt appropriate action by a government that was supposedly representing the people. Just like David Cameron Prime Minister in 2009, during a more recent so called economic crises, declaring that we were all in this together. Well we might have been in it together but everyone was clearly not 'in it' as equals.

However, halleluiah, war is declared and suddenly the unemployed can double their government funded income by the simple act of enlisting in the armed forces. Never mind that the government cared little if they lived or died, while making preparations for the later. There is a photograph of Harold, newly enlisted, looking far too young to be sent to fight. The photograph is posed in military uniform, an official photograph taken primarily as a reminder for mothers and wives of what their young sons and husbands looked like when they went to war. An obligatory photograph commissioned because, in that era before mass photography, those government officials knew that, for many of these young men, this photograph, and memories of a too short life, would be all there was for those wives and mothers in future years – all this for 14 shillings a week. Of course those who made the decision that these young men would sacrifice their lives or health for the greater good rarely made the same sacrifice themselves, for which foresight they were rewarded with rather more than 14 shillings a week.

Often, through Harold's long life, he pondered the value attributed to work. Why, he asked, when most jobs done are unnecessary, why are people exhorted to work just for the sake of working? People need jobs we are told, we need full employment, we need to create jobs, when of course this is nonsense. What people need, as Harold well knew, is not jobs but money? How Harold deplored the doctor whose main aim was to get him back to work as quickly as possible following a heart attack. The doctor knowing that he himself would be able to retire comfortably at the age of 50, after less than 30 working years, was desperate to send a 60 year old with 46 working years behind him, back to work. Why?

And why, Harold wondered, is the work of a doctor more valued than the work of a refuse collector? Without the refuse collector the comfort and health of the nation would deteriorate enormously and very rapidly and yet, as a society, we do not value our refuse collectors. Why?

Why do we not value the jobs that truly benefit society?

Now, probably more than at any other time in history, many jobs that are done are actually not necessary, people must work for the sake of working.

But Harold knew that if, as a society, we begin with a greater potential for equality we surely give everyone more equal opportunities to make of life what they will. Why not, he wondered, a citizen's wage – yes that's right, give everyone a basic wage, in return for which they have to do – well absolutely nothing if that's what they choose. A basic, guaranteed income for all citizens which would completely eliminate a need for the increasingly bizarre welfare system currently in place.

Those who choose to live frugally and take little from the world might find this citizen's wage sufficient for their needs and so choose not to engage in paid employment. This would free up jobs for those wanting a greater income. Surely people would find that they were more mobile. With people able to vote with their feet in this way wages would rise, rents would fall, working hours would decrease and, consequently, quality of life would increase. Of course, Harold knew the answer – such a system would create too much equality for the liking of those currently at the top of the tree, no doubt they suspect that it would take away their power and control. Is all power and control not based on fear? Face your fears and they are unlikely to live up to your expectations. The greatest gift is time, giving people a basic income and freeing up time like this will not cause crime and discontent. It is financial hardship and inexcusable inequality that does that.

There is a need to prevent an underclass because an underclass is of no benefit to society as a whole.

To Speak or to Keep Silent?

Letter writing – was Harold good at letter writing? Well maybe the answer to that question depends on what the recipients' expectations might have be. Letters written to children and grandchildren were so few and far between that they were practically gold dust. Harold really didn't see the point in writing letters to share trivia, he no more thought to inflict details of the minutiae of his life onto others than he wanted to hear about the minutiae of their lives. Perhaps, then, fortunate that he never embraced social media as a means of communication!

Business letters, he said, needed to be clear and to the point, concise. Don't confuse issues with frills and information that has no relevance to the matter under discussion. Business might be as simple as arranging a family visit or more complex, relating to tracking down many descendants of a recently deceased great-aunt so that the final wishes of her father's will, on hold to allow this great-aunt to live out her life in the only home she had ever known, can be dealt with. But whatever the occasion, clarity of word and expression in such communications ensures misunderstandings, be they amusing, inconvenient or disastrous, do not occur. It's all about saying what you mean and meaning what you say. Which works best, he might ask?

'We thought we might go to the restaurant for lunch, maybe on Tuesday or Thursday, I can't do Wednesday because I have to go to the dentist because my wisdom tooth is giving me a lot of trouble. Did you ever have any trouble with your wisdom teeth? And Friday is always busy, also I think that you usually do something else on Fridays, although that might be later in the day and so not likely to interfere with lunch. Anyway let me know.'

Or

'How about lunch on Tuesday?'

This is what Harold called 'cutting the waffle and twaddle', it certainly saved on ink and paper!

And so his letters to a daughter, living far across the world, consisted of cuttings from newspapers and the result - not a few paragraphs of trivia, read and discarded, but long phone conversations each week, arguing the merits or otherwise of the news in these cuttings.

Keeping a migrant informed on their homeland and sharing together a special time that was just for them.

There are other times when to keep silent may prevent harm or discomfort for others. Harold had no love for Margaret Thatcher, he knew the damage she had done to the lives of many people but he knew also that there could be no benefit, to those people or to others, from burning effigies, dancing on the grave, of someone whose day was long gone by the time of her death. There was no longer anything to be gained or lost. If what we say has no value are there times when we should, perhaps, think twice before saying it?

But sometimes, to speak is valuable and demonstrates that we are all of one world. There are times when giving to another in word or deed transcends differences to let us know that we are more the same than we are different, for we all grieve and so we all have loved. Between Heads of state, politicians, family members and friends many messages of condolence are given, some dutiful, some meaningful and some heartfelt. Harold noted, with tears in his eyes that Gordon Brown's message of condolence to David Cameron on the death of his child, fell into the latter category – the sincerity of the message was beyond doubt. A sincerity born of understanding, for Gordon Brown had also lost a child. Were the tears in Harold's eyes there because he too shared that understanding? Was his sorrow at the still-birth of his own child many years previously, with him again on that day? Did he wonder what this son would be doing had he lived? When someone dies, and especially when they die before they are old, we grieve not just for the loss of them but also we grieve for the loss of what might have been.

Harold did not utter meaningless platitudes on the early death of his son-in-law – for these are only of benefit to the speaker, not to the bereaved – they say I have spoken to you in your grief, I have taken the time and overcome my fear of loss and grief and I have spoken to you when others have turned away. But platitudes do not benefit the grieving – the grieving need us to move on from the good we think we are doing, move on and put the bereaved person first, this is about them, not about us feeling good or comfortable. This is the time to give something of ourselves, not for ourselves.

These times are not pre-ordained. None of us know when they will arrive. They come when we least expect them and so we need always to be alert to the needs of those with whom we share this world. Our initial responses may be the most influential.

Know when to speak, when to keep silent, when to stay and when to walk away.

Lunch

Lunch, a word with a very standard meaning these days, it's what we eat in the middle of the day. These days we all call our meals breakfast, lunch and, no, no we don't, lots of us call the mid-day meal dinner. So we all call our meals breakfast, lunch/dinner and – well here again differences, what do we call the evening meal – dinner, tea, supper – the only thing we can be sure of, when we talk about the evening meal is that nobody calls it lunch, except of course if its Sunday lunch in a pub 'Sunday lunch available 12-5pm'. A very common sight these days but for many families 5pm is teatime – that is, time for the main evening meal. In fact other pubs, or even the same ones on weekdays, will have 'early bird deals from 5pm', on their evening meals. What a tangle but how endlessly amusing when different worlds collide, when the midday dinner eater finds themselves expected to wait until 8pm for their main meal. Or the regular consumer of a light 'afternoon tea' finds themselves presented with stew and potatoes at 5pm.

So many people get tangled with this naming of meals, when really what matters is that everyone has sufficient food, preferably food that does no harm. Sometimes the quality of food is a matter of choice – although Harold knew that the choice was not always as free as it seems. After all, since his youth a whole industry has grown up devoted to persuading people that they would prefer to eat foods offering little nutrition but high profit margins to the producer, rather than doing something as basic as cooking porridge, or potatoes and vegetables. Breakfast cereals were a frequent subject for Harold's incredulity, 'how can you take something basic, healthy, inexpensive, and turn it into something vastly expensive and far less healthy', well of course the answer is simple, manufacturers make money that way. Rice retails at about 50 pence a kilo, puffed up, with added salt and sugar, and packaged as breakfast cereal it retails at £6.50 a kilo. And another whole industry has grown up trying to persuade people to 'eat healthily' and so the cycle continues. Even in the basics Harold observed great differences over his lifetime, noting that 'the bread you can buy is all pretty dire these days', and so, with the aid of a bread maker, taking up the making of his own bread at the age of 89.

He observed on more than one occasion, as he examined the contents of the donation box for the local food bank, 'If you want to help someone who doesn't have enough to eat why would you give them huge bottles of coke or lemonade?' That's not food, that's not nutrition, that's just something to slowly kill them. Although, of course, not everyone sees it that way – the more gullible trust that medical science and the very rapidly disintegrating National Health Service will step in to put their bodies right again.

And the endless tins of basics baked beans in the food bank collections – that's not generosity, that's salving your conscience, you've given something, but it perpetuates the myth of the undeserving poor – well its good enough for them, beggars can't be choosers, and other such platitudes.

How has food become so complicated and yet so simplified? The traditional British cooked breakfast. Bacon, sausages, tomatoes, mushrooms, eggs, where did that idea come from? The average British person has never sat down each, or indeed any, morning to such a meal. Back in Harold's 1920's childhood sometimes home cured bacon with bread and perhaps an egg if the hens were laying, but mostly porridge, or bread.

Now we have, in pubs and cafes across the country, 'The Ploughman's Lunch', cheese ploughman's, ham ploughman's, even scotch egg ploughman's or quiche ploughman's. In earlier times, when the job of ploughman still existed, a ploughman was poor, really poor usually, he had no land of his own, depended on someone else needing his labour, so a ploughman's lunch, if he was lucky, would be bread and cheese, perhaps some pickle and an apple, old and wrinkled from long storage by the spring.

The farmer meanwhile, was often more comfortably off, he could perhaps afford to pay for the labour of the ploughman. He could keep, feed, kill and cure a pig or two to provide a little meat for his family, while the gentleman was affluent, he could afford for others to raise the meat he would eat and he could buy his meat without regard for how the rest of the animal would be used. Inns and hostelries in market towns, in those days when the food they provided catered more for need than desire, would provide the ploughman's lunch of bread, cheese and pickle, the farmer's lunch of bread, ham, cheese and pickle and the gentleman's lunch of roast beef, bread, cheese and pickle, catering not so much for all tastes, but for all but the emptiest of purses.

Although Harold probably didn't call it lunch, after all growing up in Lancashire during the 1920's and 1930's lunch was the name for a mid-morning drink and maybe a snack.

I Love You Because

In this world we are many people, we all have our quirks, our likes, our dislikes but it is the love of others, when that love doesn't doubt us, when it gives us a helping hand and when it makes our hearts lighter and our futures brighter, that sees us through. Harold understood that what truly matters is not academic, financial or career achievements but the ability to be happy and in harmony with those with whom we share our lives, both at home and in the wider world.

Harold used many ways to show his love and we loved him most of all for being him.

Love

How do we show that we love our children? In the hurried 'love you loads', or 'love you to the moon and back' or other platitudes tossed over the shoulder to them as real life calls from the other side of the school or nursery door? Maybe that shows love and maybe it sometimes, perhaps, is also a way of appeasing guilt at needing to leave those children in the care of others, or guilt at feeling relief at being able to do so. Well, that's one kind of love and there is, as we all know, more than one kind of love. When Harold was tied to working, to earning a living, did he ever wish he could spend more time with his children? Was he pleased to be able to provide for them well enough that they never knew how little spare money there was? And did he show his real love for each of his children in a myriad of ways? Ways that made it about them and not about him proving his love to the world?

Here are some ways in which Harold showed his love.

Insisting on coming out of hospital sooner than he should have done so that he could spend the days before Christmas Day in the cold, dark, damp cellar finishing dolls' houses for two excited little girls, who only knew of the sacrifice he had made years later, told to them by someone else.

Holding close a sick child, instinctively knowing that physical closeness was the comfort needed, wrapping the child in his heavy overcoat so that he didn't have to leave her to fetch a blanket, knowing that the comfort was needed right then, and giving it without question.

Spending time each week identifying news items that would interest an adult child in order to keep alive a relationship across half the world and half a lifetime. Even at the age of 97 when many people would have thought that he had earned the right to receive, more than to give, his giving a silent testimonial to his love, a constant unspoken reminder of the value of the relationship to them both.

Showing sincerity of feeling. Truly shown in the simplicity through which it was expressed. No throw away compliments dispensed at each meeting but real compliments simply given on rare occasions that showed a genuine pleasure or liking and were the more valued for that. That's how we knew he truly appreciated, enjoyed or loved something or someone with more than a run of the mill pleasure, and his word for this was 'like'. 'I like your outfit', so rarely heard as to be truly meaningful. 'I like it' expressed with a smile after a very careful scrutiny of estate agents particulars for a house to be bought. And perhaps most special of all, in his advanced years when staying away from home was increasingly difficult for him, when he had made the almost herculean effort to do so for Christmas, the 'I've liked being here', volunteered upon his departure.

Teaching the art of respect, even though, with the natural belligerence of teenagers eager to make their own impression on the world, his children fought against it, wondering out loud why music should be played quietly enough not to disturb others, why chores had to be completed at a required time. Of course, eventually they would all leave the family home, all leave overnight the greasy dishes waiting to be washed, and all experience the despair of coming the next morning, already late for work, into a kitchen full of the dirty dishes. Sometimes the things we learn in our early years suddenly make sense to us much later in life.

Love is something we feel, it is often best expressed in thought and deeds more so than in words.

Eggs

'Duck eggs' Harold said when given the larger than average, tinged with blue but still uncommonly white, eggs to examine, 'don't see those so much these days, not now the eggs are all mass produced for the supermarkets'. He examined them carefully, handling the delicate eggs with the ease of someone experienced in the art of egg handling. Was he remembering, more than half a century before, collecting still warm eggs from nesting boxes? Who taught him to scoop and lift the eggs, to let them nestle in the cupped palm of his hand and so avoid breaking the soft, delicate new-laid shells? Did he, a couple of years later, as the by then experienced egg collector, show his younger sister how to scoop and lift equally gently? Was he impatient with her early efforts or did he use the same gentle encouragement his mother had used with him? Of course we only surmise that his mother taught through gentle encouragement, or even that it was indeed his mother who taught him, but that is because we like to glorify the mothers of the past as always kind, gentle and caring, with endless time for their children. But, for Harold's mother, maybe those were the days immediately following the death of a subsequent child, after a life of six weeks. Was she exhausted from managing the house and the needs of her living child while recovering from childbirth and grieving for her dead baby? Was she sometimes overly harsh with him in those days? After all he was alive and thriving while his brother was not. In later years, when his own first son was still-born did his thoughts go back to his mother? Did he grieve then for what might have been, not only for his son but for his brother?

But back to the eggs.

'Not the best for eating though, ducks are like foxes – and people - they're scavengers, they eat anything, that doesn't make for good eggs, goodness knows what's in them.'

But that's probably not the main reason for the limited quantities of duck eggs in our supermarkets. In fact ducks aren't good sitters, they don't have the devotion to their eggs that hens and many other birds have. Actually they have an alarming tendency to abandon their new laid eggs, perhaps thinking that in laying the egg they have done their duty and now the egg can take care of itself – continuing the age old argument about when an offspring is ready to be independent, although the duck may be pushing the limits somewhat in believing that its unhatched ducklings can manage alone.

'We used to put the duck eggs under the hens', Harold recalled, 'hens are very good sitters, very patient waiting for the eggs to hatch'. So sometimes patience really is a virtue. 'When they hatch the ducklings just follow the hen around, finding food like she does.'

When the duck eggs hatch the hen, knowing that she has hatched these eggs, is unperturbed by her oversized babies and clucks around them, keeping them safe and teaching them how to peck food from the ground– until the dramatic day when the ducklings find the pond. This part of the story always amused Harold, even when he told it many years later to his grandchildren. This is the part of the story where the ducklings quack loudly and race to the water, abandoning their foster mother without a backward glance, taking to their new wet world like – well – like ducks to water, this they don't need to be taught, they just know how to swim and how to find food in the water. They swim and splash, quaking gleefully, while the hen watches from the pond's edge, frantically calling for her babies because hens, she knows, don't swim, now she is really confused, surely her babies will come to harm? How soon before she forgets these treacherous ducklings and lays eggs of her own to raise chicks? Or do the people fool her again sliding yet more duck eggs under her, taking advantage of her natural inclination to care, the archetypal mother hen clucking over the young even when they are not her own.

Farming

'The best days of my life those were'. A chance remark made one day during Harold's very long retirement, referring to the time in his childhood spent living on a farm. He saw the farm again once, many years after he had first left it, the house now gone and the land less loved. It grieved him that those who had the care of this land in more recent years did not care for it. Simple, basic errors in land management which he epitomised through the obvious failure to plant trees. On that visit it was abundantly clear that, as the old trees had died and fallen, no thought had been given to the long term effects and no replacement trees planted. Once all the old trees were gone the now windswept land had taken on an unloved, barren aspect. There is unspoken belief by those in control of a national economy whose government continually demands more for less, that the land will continue to give even if corners and costs are cut, and care is not given. It will not.

When does one become a farmer? When one farms the land to increasingly relentless and unsustainable demands or when one understands that the needs of the land and the livestock are paramount to ensuring good quality production? When one understands that quality outstrips quantity every time? These days quality is marketed as 'artisan', 'designer', it costs more because this is the true cost of food. These days 'artisan' means 'we care'. We care for the life of the land, for the lives, and deaths, of the livestock and for the lives of the people. Surely one is only truly a farmer if one farms the land with such care?

Well, Harold learnt some things from his time on the farm which he liked to share. Probably he learnt much more than he ever told because he never set out to instruct. The knowledge that he did share emerged in conversations, some of them 80 years after he left the land, but still pertinent.

Cows

Cows like to be outside, except in very cold weather. Cows produce better milk if they live outside. It costs more to produce good quality milk than to produce poor quality milk. If a community wants milk and dairy products, that community really needs to eat beef or veal, or at least have a ready market for beef and veal because approximately 50% of calves born are male. Male calves do not contribute to the dairy industry. They need to be raised for meat or else killed at birth. There are almost 2 million dairy cows in the UK, the corresponding number of heifers or bulls cannot be kept as pets, a farmer attempting to do this would very quickly run out of grazing land.

Cows, in order to keep producing milk, need to calve every second year. Spontaneous abortion in a herd means a loss of potential revenue for the farmer, keeping a donkey or two in with pregnant cattle helps to prevent spontaneous abortion. These days there is research to supposedly support or refute such understandings but back in Harold's days on the farm this was old wisdom, passed between generations.

Donkeys

Donkeys, therefore, are valuable but remember that donkeys are desert animals, they don't do well in damp and freezing weather conditions. Donkeys, contrary to popular depictions, are not actually stubborn or stupid, but they do think for themselves, just like cats. If they want to do what you are asking of them they will do it, if they don't want to then you have to make it attractive to them because, unlike dogs and horses, they have no particular desire to please humans. Donkeys are happy to coexist with people but, to give their best, require a mutually acceptable contract – they really are very much like people.

Hares

How many times in a lifetime do people see hares in the wild? Those who live close to the countryside may see them occasionally, especially if they know where and when to look, but many people these days will never see a hare in the wild. Harold and his childhood friends knew where to look – in the potato fields, because hares don't burrow underground like rabbits, they sleep and raise their young in an open 'forms', choosing naturally sheltered locations. Rows of well grown potato plants, with their furrows and ridges designed to increase the growing depth for the potato plants, provide safe resting places and a degree of security for young hares. By the time the potatoes are harvested the young are ready to move on. Did Harold and his friends go looking for them sometimes, maybe to spot the babies, huddled, waiting for the adults to return? Of course in his childhood the potatoes were harvested by hand, giving the hares plenty of time to make their getaway, and the children plenty of opportunities to watch them, although maybe some didn't make it and ended up simmering with carrots and turnips in a farmhouse or cottage.

Lettuce

Of course, for many people these days seasonal food is a little understood concept. A lack of understanding driven not only by remoteness from the land and food production but, less forgivably, by the supermarkets relentless desire to make people buy everything all year round. Market gardens cover acres of land in poly-tunnels so that they can meet supermarket demand for strawberries and salad crops in December. But in Harold's youth demand was more greatly consumer led and shops were small. No point harvesting boxes full of lettuce on damp chilly summer days, they wouldn't sell, but make sure there were plenty harvested and quickly into town on days that promised to be warm and sunny. Of course no long range weather forecasts then, the farmers had to be their own decision makers and their own meteorologists. Their livelihoods might depend on that knowledge passed down to them from previous generations, which direction to look for the approaching weather, signs given by plants and animals that good or bad weather was approaching. And ever guessing, would that mist lift to give a glorious sunny day or would this be the day it stayed, lingering dank and dismal throughout the day? Would it be a stew day or a salad day?

What makes a farmer? Is it what they know and how they use what they know? Is it knowing that the land is there for the long haul and a part of their job is to protect and nurture it for future generations of farmers?

The Gardener

Harold professed himself to be 'not a gardener'. By which, it seems, he meant that he had never pursued any depth of knowledge, had never deliberately made the move to find out more but that didn't prevent him learning something about gardening, and later sharing that learning with others. Although he didn't express it in these terms, he clearly knew that successful learning depended on successful teaching.

Harold frequently recalled differences in the teaching ability of the teachers he encountered during his short time at grammar school, for their impact on him was great. The History teacher, still fascinated by his subject after years of teaching, eager to share his fascination with his students. An engaging and informative teacher, caring not for covering a syllabus and ticking off targets reached, but caring that his students should have a valuable experience to take forward into their lives. Wanting to foster a love of finding out more, of looking more deeply into subjects, in order to give greater pleasure to their working lives, their later retirements and, although this master of his subject would not have known it at the time, to get them through whatever trials the forthcoming war had in store for each. Or the mathematics teacher, because this was the days before the very serious subject of mathematics was transformed into the more insignificant 'maths', who bored his students with 'endless droning'. Only those with keen minds, a will to learn the subject or a natural aptitude, acquired a sound working knowledge of this subject. How many futures did this poor teaching influence?

This much Harold knew – being 'good' at your subject, a world expert even, does not necessarily equip you to be able to share that knowledge with others – it doesn't make you a teacher in any true sense of the word. But he knew that the world is full of skilled teachers supporting eager, engaged learners outside the confines of those institutions dedicated to education. He knew that we all learn from others we meet and it is for us to make what we will of the learning, to follow the good, to follow the bad, to seek the knowledge we want or need. To store the knowledge we don't want or need right now against a time when we might need it. In this way we all have the means to acquire much knowledge and many skills, wherever we are and whatever we do.

Which brings us back to gardening. Harold didn't label himself as a gardener. Quite the opposite. 'I'm not a gardener', those were his words, but, over the many years of his life, he acquired snippets and blocks of knowledge relating to plants and growing. This was his horticultural learning. He had many teachers through books, newspapers, magazines, television programmes, conversations with others, not forgetting those who taught him simply because he watched them. When we don't watch other people we lose opportunities to learn from them. In later life, when his sense of smell was almost gone and he could no longer easily detect the fragrance of flowers, Harold recalled with pleasure, summer evenings walking by a garden close to his childhood home, a garden with a twenty foot long flowerbed, acknowledging the dedication of the gardener who each year filled the surrounding air with glorious mingling flower scents for those passing by to enjoy.

This much at least he knew about gardening

Sweet peas can be grown up through runner beans. This way you can enjoy the sweet pea flowers while the beans quietly go about growing tender and delicious early pickings or big, strong pods, fat with beans. Left to ripen these give dried beans for winter cooking, or for next year's seeds. But if you swop some seeds with a neighbour next year's plants will be stronger than if you continually use your own seeds. Think ahead though, if you want a really good crop dig a deep trench in the autumn and spend the winter months filling it with – well, with anything that will rot away over the winter. Most plants won't grow in overworked soil but they give and they take. The beans will take all the nutrition they need from your rotted waste and in return they will put nitrogen into the earth to feed your cabbages next season. Think before you plant with Harold's wise words, 'you can't just shove things in anywhere and expect them to do well'.

If you grow tomatoes in grow bags that's not the end of the story. Once your tomato plants are finished put some lettuce seeds in the grow bag, they'll do fine there. Of course you have to care for the tomatoes, with feeding and regular watering, otherwise the skins will split the moment there's heavy rain.

If plants like where you've put them, or where the wind or the birds have put them, they'll grow and flourish, if you put them where they don't like to be they won't – just like people really except that plants can't tell you in words if something is wrong. You have to watch them, if you get it wrong remember what they have taught you – and use that teaching wisely next time.

For a man who was not given to wasting money, who recognised that vast amounts of 'tat' are manufactured and marketed to the unwary who truly believe the advertising that tells them their lives will be infinitely better with it, even if they need to borrow money to pay for it, his words reflected perhaps where his true passions lay. Telling us to 'plant thyme around the garden hut, it'll smell good when you pass it', rather than questioning the decision to spend a very large sum of money on the garden hut. Did he know or guess the hours of pleasure the hut would give? Did it recall for him some past garden or countryside spot used for his own escape from the cares of a childhood cut short by the death of his father? Some things we will never know, we all take secrets with us when we go.

Food that is grown with care and respect will always be superior in taste to that which is mass produced, even if it's just a cabbage. In Harold's youth the greengrocers sold strawberries picked that morning, any left the next day were sold half price as 'jam strawberries', now the supermarkets sell strawberries all year round – how can that be better, no anticipation, no thrill of finding the first strawberries of the season – maybe it's all part of a greater plan, give them strawberries in January and they'll be placid and compliant.

Your hanging baskets won't survive three days without water in the summer.

Very late in life, in a neighbourhood of neat front gardens, Harold paid someone to care for his own tiny front garden, to mow the grass, trim the edges, pull the weeds and tend the plants growing in borders around the edges. The gardener employed actually sent 'a young lad' - Harold frequently used the phrases of his northern youth throughout his 60 years further south - who knew nothing about gardening except how to operate the lawn mower and how to trim lawn edges. When Harold showed this young lad which were the weeds to pull and which the plants to leave he taught and the young lad learnt, eagerly as it happens, so that over time the young lad trusted himself to make the right decisions for the garden.

Knowledge passed on, successful teaching, knowledge absorbed, valued learning.

Charity and Benevolence

Some dictionary definitions:

- *Benevolent* - wishing to do good; actively friendly and helpful; charitable.

- *Charitable* – generous in giving to those in need.

- *Need* – stand in want of; require.

- *Want* – to be without or fall short of; lack; be deficient; poverty.

And some things Harold couldn't fathom.

Why do the powers that be in his local council have so little regard for the users of the food bank that the only place made available for its location is a cellar? Indeed so little concern is there for the users of this food bank that it is almost inaccessible for many people, for those with mobility problems, sight problems, with children in prams. Why is it made so difficult for them that they have to ask someone else to accompany them, or ask someone else to mind their children while they go for their handouts?

How greatly Harold applauded actions he heard about in other countries such as the Seychelles, where all pregnant women received the basics of cooking oil, powdered milk and rice. Freely available to every pregnant woman regardless of her situation and so there was no stigma in the collecting and receiving, a right not a charity handout.

Why is it that so many people not only want to do good but want also to ensure that their goodness is seen and attributed to them – is it not enough to have helped someone? Must charitable actions be as much about the giver as about the receiver?

Harold never understood why so much help must be charity, or why that charity has to be about the recipient continuing to have less than the giver. Why can charity not enable the recipient to be the equal of the giver? In his middle years the local church held, every year, a Christmas tree service during which the children of church going families took a wrapped gift to be placed under the tree and later passed to 'needy' children. Why, Harold questioned, were used and unwanted toys requested? Why he wondered were those 'needy' children not deemed worthy to have new toys at Christmas? Well it's because that's charity, if the child receiving has new toys they become the equal of the child giving but that must not be allowed to happen because that is sharing, not charity. But really! How generous is it to give only that which is no longer wanted by yourself or your child? When they contribute to food bank collections how many people add the better quality items that they, themselves, will eat and how many make special purchases of cheap baked beans, fizzy drinks, multi-packs of crisps – look how generous I am. True giving is not charity it's not about how much you give but how much you share of what you have.

Harold understood that sharing brings respect, ultimately it may not bring equality but it brings respect. He liked that his children attended a comprehensive school, saying he liked that, 'the bin man's daughter sits down next to the Doctor's daughter'. So although this didn't address the inequalities in other areas of their lives it gave them a chance to know each other, to share their education. It maybe gave the bin man's daughter a fighting chance, even though the odds were stacked against her, and if she were to make the academic achievements that her middle class peers took for granted she would need much greater powers of resilience, of determination, of willingness to overcome other's expectations. Hers would be a much longer and deeper journey into realms unknown than that of her middle class peers.

On what was to be, although we didn't know it at the time, Harold's final excursion into the world that was not hospital, his giving was refused. Seeing a charity collecting at the supermarket door, he looked for the familiar sight of a collection tin for people passing to put their spare change in. No tin could be seen. He spoke to the young man representing the charity, with the few pounds change from his shopping in his hand, offering the young man his donation. 'Where shall I put this, I want to donate it to your charity?' But no says the young man we do not want your anonymous donation we want your bank details, we don't take cash, we only want that you set up a direct debit. Really we are saying to you that your donation is not good enough for us, we are demanding that to support our charity you do it only this way, we need your name, you can no longer give anonymously, and we expect that you will go on giving, each month the same amount. We, the recipients of your giving want to be in control of your giving.

 How much did they lose that day, and subsequent days at different supermarkets in different towns, as those willing to give a couple of pounds as a random donation refused to sign up to controlled giving? Remember, those who collect for charities, you may tell us we must do it this way, or that way, but ultimately we can simply take our charitable giving elsewhere, we can control our giving.

Harold's intended giving was benevolent, he wished to do good, to be helpful, to be charitable, and to give anonymously. On this occasion, his benevolence was rejected because he would not put his name to his giving or to be compelled into future giving.

Quality

A young soldier in 1945 Harold, 25 years old, had just spent four years of his life on what was, from some perspectives, a fruitless endeavour. He had survived, mostly physically intact and without the deep mental scars from an earlier war that had led to his own father's suicide in 1934, or indeed the scars of war that had led to his son-in-law's suicide in 2001. Another conflict, another country and another unnecessarily early death. The war Harold had been dragged into followed 'the Great War, the war to end all wars'. How inappropriately called was that war? And how many conflicts have followed? But we digress. In later times, with decades for reflection behind him, Harold would still affirm that conflict could be resolved without this mass destruction. He saw Dresden near this time, a beautiful city destroyed in an act of spite and vengeance, lives lost, lives destroyed, childhood dreams and ambitions cut short – just as his own had been with his father's death, and he knew that this was not the way.

Harold knew, he always knew, that however great, small or seemingly insurmountable the conflict, the power of communication, of talk, of compromise, of respect for others, of understanding of difference, could be used to negotiate and, indeed, despite all the killing and destruction, talk is what it came down to. The war was not ended by bombing Dresden.

But now we digress even further. In 1945 Harold is just a young soldier, in Belgium, waiting to go home, waiting to be released from the military, waiting to start his life. He is safe, war has ended, peace treaties have been signed and demands upon his time are no longer all consuming, no more packing up and moving in the middle of the night with two minutes notice, no more ten minute meal stops on long marches, wishing the lights were out so that he couldn't see, as well as taste, the food – if such a word can be used to describe some of the meals eaten in this way. This day he is, for an hour or two at least, free and he walks through the streets of a small Belgian town with a friend. Another young man, who if the world had not taken such a wild course of action, Harold probably would never have met. Harold knows him as Jock, he also knows his family name but in later years this is an unnecessary addition to the story and so he just says, 'I knew him as Jock', silently acknowledging that was not the name given to him at birth. What did he know Harold as?

It is morning, but not early morning, the town is awake, it must not be too cold for windows and doors are open and people see the two young men passing by. As they pass one house, the man – we don't know his name – greets them, he knows they are British from their uniforms and their very presence in the town at that point in time. Harold and Jock respond, exchanging greetings, probably in English because, then as now, the British education system did not value the learning of the languages of our neighbours sufficiently and so it is only in the years following, when Harold married a Flemish woman and spent time in Belgium as a civilian, that he begin to learn how to use this other language.

The man asks a question, 'Will you come into the house and share a drink with my wife and I?'

The dilemma – In English when we hear phrases such as, 'I want to share a drink with you', or, 'will you take a drink with me?' these phrases say to us now, and in 1945, that you are being invited to partake of an alcoholic drink. When Harold heard this phrase thoughts raced through his head, at the time these must have been flashes but later, when he tells the story, these are articulated in more detail. Harold knows that Jock shares his thoughts on war and neither has any wish to cause offence. Harold knows that Jock is a Scottish Presbyterian who doesn't drink alcohol and yet it cannot be all down to Harold as Jock sits politely by because Harold has been raised Methodist and also does not drink alcohol. Probably Jock has similar thoughts to Harold's flashing through his mind, perhaps he also, in later years shared this story with his children and grandchildren, a shared memory spreading through different families.

In the space of a moment, with no more than a quick glance between them, a decision must be made. What can they do but thank the man and follow him into his house, into the kitchen.

Here, as the story is told to children and grandchildren, imagination must take over, because Harold's story has a precise focus and, just like the few letters he wrote, his telling of the story cut out unnecessary detail. And so we imagine – the sun shining through a small window and a patch of sunlight on the floor where the sun has also crept through the open door. A small kitchen range for cooking as well as to provide heat and hot water when needed. Little in the way of food supplies, war has just ended, the rationing and shortages of food experienced by people in Britain look positively feast-like to those who have experienced the war in occupied countries, but possibly the window gives view of a small garden with vegetables growing, each plant carefully tended to prevent another hungry day. There are no luxuries, no processed or imported foodstuffs – the cupboard really is bare. Harold and Jock greet the woman that they meet in the kitchen and she welcomes them enthusiastically. Although her husband tells her, in the Flemish that they do not yet understand, why he has invited them in, she already knows, for this is an act that they have planned together from the beginning of the occupation. From the moment, in 1940, when they sealed the tin and stored it on the top shelf of the kitchen cupboard, 'To share with the first Englishman to pass in peacetime'. An act of deep faith that their country would one day be liberated, that peace would come, that if they held out long enough they could live their lives again.

The woman invites Harold and Jock to sit, in 1945 this kitchen is her domain and only she has the power to make visitors feel truly welcome here, she is smiling, they are both very, very pleased to bring these two young men into their home, to share this moment with them.

The woman goes to the cupboard and takes down the sealed tin, nothing is hurried – there is the anticipation of years of peace ahead, there is no need to hurry. Besides, doing this well is much more important than doing it quickly. From the tin she takes something Harold and Jock have never seen before, they look like seeds or beans, they are white. She sets a small, heavy iron pan on the heat of the range and puts the white beans into it to roast very slowly. Now they know what these beans are because now they can smell the aroma of coffee.

Do they both, Harold and Jock, at this moment experience the same emotions? Relief that they are not to be offered alcohol, pleasure in the smell of the coffee – actually Harold, and possibly Jock, both being children of the poverty stricken interwar years, have never smelt fresh coffee being roasted before. What passed for coffee in their childhood communities was that fearsome concoction sold as 'camp coffee' which, in his telling of this story Harold would label as 'dreadful stuff, absolutely dreadful stuff'.

The woman carefully grinds the roasted coffee beans, using, of course because this is 1945, a hand grinder mounted on a small wooden box, filling the kitchen still further with the coffee's aroma, even before the careful and slow brewing process commences.

The coffee pot comes to the table before the coffee is poured into what? China cups with saucers, tin mugs? We don't know because this fact is irrelevant, what is in the cup or mug is infinitely more important than the vessel which holds it.

As they drink the coffee this becomes the moment when two young men, products of the cheap food expectations that have resulted in Britain following the repeal of the Corn Laws in 1846, recognise that quality in food can be respected and valued. One cup of freshly prepared coffee beats a lifetime of camp coffee and they both understand the enormity of the act of saving these coffee beans throughout the war, and the value of the sharing that they have been a part of on this day. Indeed so great is the impact of this encounter

73

that Harold will still tell the story to his grandchildren in his 97th

year.

The Party's Over

From when we are born, and no matter how solitary a person we imagine ourselves to be, we all travel together with others through the best of life, the worst of life and everything in between. When one of us dies the party, as we knew it, is indeed over and we have all to rearrange ourselves in a new order, to form a different party from where we continue our lives. This we do each time our party is broken, for life is about endings as well as beginnings and without death there can be no life, without endings there can be no new beginnings.

Against all the odds – 98

How does it feel to approach your 98th birthday? An age that nothing in Harold's family history or his own life would have led him to expect to reach. Popular opinion tends to the celebration of the long lives of others but is there a point at which the difficulties of coping with the demands of life exceed the joy in living? Some people, of course, willingly declare these difficulties to anyone who will listen, expressing their need to be gone from the world, while their families relish the fame that an extremely aged relative brings to them. But Harold – we don't know. In his last years he increasingly tried to prepare his family for the inevitable, 'something will get me soon', 'I might not be here then', 'after I'm gone', but we largely ignored these, after all, he had always been there why would he not continue to be there, next week, next year, forever.

But what we don't know is how Harold felt – how often is that the case? When someone asks how we feel how often do we temper our reply to how we think they want us to feel? Especially if how we truly feel is likely to cause that other person distress, to perhaps destroy illusions they may hold, or to bring into question something that they hold dear. And how often do we not say things, not express opinions, not question or criticise because to do these things would be to cause hurt, upset or distress to another. We know our nearest and dearest well but never really know everything of them, some things we don't share.

There is a horror to being very elderly and in hospital and some of this horror Harold shared in passing comments but the endurance of his final days in hospital must largely have been a solitary and unspoken horror.

'Did you ring the bell' we ask seeing him in distress and needing help with personal care, 'yes', he answers, ' but nobody comes', and we see this for ourselves when we ring the bell on his behalf and nobody comes for twenty minutes. A man with an enlarged prostate cannot wait 20 minutes to urinate. 'You haven't drunk your water', we say, 'No', he replies,' I can't reach it, they put it too far away 'and we see this for ourselves. We see these things not once, but over and over again – a lack of basic care that would be called by its name if this was a child – neglect – an acknowledged form of abuse. And here, in a hospital staffed with trained professionals, not abuse born of a lack of knowledge but abuse born of a lack of respect and care, intentional abuse that so often goes unchecked, especially when it involves the very elderly, for the dead do not tell tales.

But right to the end Harold observed what was happening around him, he stored fragments of information and put these together to create nuggets of knowledge to share with family members on their long hospital visits. He noted how skilled staff of one nationality were in providing nursing care and how fluent staff of another nationality were in the English language despite it not being their first language. He noted that staff of these two nationalities, when working together, were best able to interpret and meet his needs, often better than more senior staff who shared both his nationality and his first language. Is it empathy that makes us one world?

And Harold – well right to the end of his 98 years he was a great respecter of quality of life in all its forms, for all people. From him we know that small things matter, even the quality of the food provided for elderly hospital patients. On the day before his death Harold declared the hospital soup to be 'very borderline'. Even then, when he knew he was dying and that any one of the tiny meals he ate

might be his last, even then the quality of that food mattered.

Earliest Memories

It is said that children don't remember their earliest days but there is no firm consensus on when people do start remembering, or being able to recall, specific events or feelings. How do we measure and how do we assess people's memories for accuracy? Well the truth is these things are not really possible but still many people do set great store by 'my earliest memory'. Actually people can get very competitive about this, they all seem to want their earliest memory to be from the earliest age, probably some people actually claim to remember being born, or being in the womb – people really are very competitive. In truth it's most likely that earliest experiences build to lasting memories, to feelings of warmth, comfort and security for the lucky ones or to fear, hunger and pain for the least lucky. Does either of these alone support a child's development into a caring community member, alert to the needs of others as well as self? Or is that best achieved through comfort and security interspersed with smaller elements of fear and anxiety thus enabling the child to learn how to cope with both the good and the bad that life will bring them. Is this how our children best develop empathy for the situations of others? Is this how we become a caring society? Harold knew that those suffering adversity weren't helped by a welfare system that marked them as other, as less, as a sub-species, he knew that, while some may have a greater cushioning and a longer fall time, a fall from grace could happen to anyone because, one way or another we are all dependent on the will and actions of others. He knew that if we really want to help people back into work when they had been struck by adversity then we, as a society, need to give them the means to help themselves and yes, that would mean giving them sufficient money to go out into the world with grace, dignity and self-belief.

One day, as a married man with four children to support, Harold came across a young man, unemployed and in search of a job, we don't know how the encounter came about, was it someone he saw regularly on the bus or near his place of work? This we don't know, we don't know much actually because, not one to shout about his own good deeds, he only seems to have told this story once. Speaking with the young man he discovered that the young man was eager to apply for a job he had seen advertised, a job that had fired his enthusiasm and excitement, getting this job would give him security, pride, give back meaning to his life, give him the means to get married and raise a family; but the young man had not the required suit for the interview. Did Harold hesitate before he offered the young man a loan? Certainly this was not a usual action, he had little enough money to spare at that time in his life and didn't know the young man well, but trusting to instinct and perhaps seeing that a greater good could be served by his action he offered the young man a loan to buy or hire, we don't know which, a suit for the interview. A week later he saw the young man again, 'thank you', said the young man, 'I got the job'. We don't know if the money was repaid. That wasn't a part of this story.

We digress for that was nobody's earliest memory. However, as with many families, or groups of friends or colleagues, earliest memories were shared and two of Harold's come easily to mind but even for him it was not possible to identify which of these is the earlier memory. However, one would have been a daily occurrence while the other was a one off momentous occasion. One was embedded into his consciousness over time and the other had a more sudden and sharp impact on memory and remembrances, but they both give a glimpse of a past age, an age experienced at the start of what would, against all the odds, turn out to be a very long life.

'One of my earliest memories is watching my father going to the well and drawing two buckets of water for my mother to use during the day.'

From this we know that even the basics in life required physical effort, how carefully did his mother use that water each day to avoid another trip to the well because in fact drawing water from a well is hard work, drawing water from a well and carrying that water back home is even harder pregnant and with a toddler in tow.

From this we know that his father was considerate, doing this task to save his wife a job in those days when running any house was mostly 'donkey work'.

His second memory, 'Being lifted up at the dockside to see the big ship sailing'. We don't know who lifted him, his father? His mother? One of the other relatives there on this momentous day to say goodbye to his Aunty as she left for a new life in Canada. Back then in the early 1920's those who went to the docks that day would not have expected to see her again in their lifetime, well most of them would have had that thought but probably not him. At two or three years of age almost certainly his greatest excitement that day would be seeing the big ship and watching it sail, how good that someone thought to show him, when they might easily have ignored him in their own sorrow at the sister they were losing.

He met this aunty once again, more than half a century later, when she paid her only visit back to England. By then elderly and a widow, with a lifetime of working behind her. Who could have known that when she sailed from the dock that day, her young husband by her side, filled with optimism for their new life in Canada, who could have known that an accident on the ship would leave her husband an invalid, unable to work. How little any of us know of what is in store for us. We none of us know what is around the next corner but, like explorers, we mostly keep on going until we find out. Then we deal with it and move on to the next corner. Except for those who sometimes opt out of the exploration and stagnate in what we call by names such as depression, idleness, slothfulness, mental illness – when maybe, in reality, all that's happened is that they've already been round too many corners, maybe they just need a break from the unpredictability of corners, maybe they need some straight lines for a while. After all, straight lines build memories just like corners do.

Horses

Harold had no sentimentality towards animals, no desire to love and cherish a pet cat or dog but, at the same time, far more respect for animals than many of the 'devoted' pet owners of the modern age. House cats, house rabbits, what's that all about? Who imagined that a cat or a rabbit would prefer to live indoors? To have a cat around the house, the yard, the garden was almost a necessity in Harold's younger days but the cat had a job to do in keeping the house free from mice and other vermin. In return for doing their job well nobody bothered them over much as they spent the vast majority of their days seeking out warm fires and stoves to sleep beside, or sunny spots to bask in. Perhaps they also served as playmate, comforter and confidante to various family members in quiet moments, because many cats, being sociable animals in the wild who live in family groups, seem naturally amenable to human contact. It's strange the things that people readily remember. In Harold's final years an elderly family friend, much of her recent years lost to her own memory forever, recalled with clarity always having a cat on her lap as a child, recalled also her mother's continual protestations to her to put the cat down and do something useful. Did she do so? Willingly, reluctantly, for just long enough to send her mother's attentions elsewhere, then back to her cat? We don't know for this memory was just a brief glimpse into her long past childhood.

Harold tolerated with remarkably good grace the clear affection that his children had for the family cat. A cat who had the good sense not to let Harold find her sleeping on the beds and who quickly relinquished her place on an armchair if he approached looking intent on sitting there. She understood him as much as he understood her, his insistence that the cat went out at night, in those days before cat flaps in doors and windows, was really for her benefit because, despite the protestations of his children at the thought of their cat spending the night outdoors, he knew that she would prefer that to the alternative of being shut in all night.

There was a dog as well, somebody must have worked hard to persuade Harold of the need to keep a family dog. A pet dog! This really was outside his understanding, dogs were working animals, just like horses. A guard dog, chained outside, a sheepdog, a guide dog, a hunting dog, all kept and cared for because they did a job. He never could understand the thinking behind spending more than the value of the animal on vet's bills. Dogs, horses, cows – if the bill exceeded the animal's value it was surely money wasted, or else a rich person's plaything. A guard dog or a mouser cat were easily replaced and so had little intrinsic value, a sheep dog, with its many hours of training and devotion to a working partnership – much less easily replaced. Its consequent greater value usually earning it a prime place by the fireside at the end of the day. But because he knew that times had changed and because he loved his children, a pet dog there was.

Horses, of course, were seen in abundance in Harold's early 20th century childhood. They worked the farms and carted heavy loads, they provided in other ways too and many a young town dwelling child would be sent out into the street with shovel and bucket to collect manure for the garden. But horses, like dogs, were working animals, some more easily replaced than others and so of greater value, but all to be treated with respect, valued for their contributions to the wellbeing of the people they shared their lives with.

When your horses represent your livelihood why would you oblige them to work beyond their capabilities? Surely your aim would be to keep them productive for as long as possible, by treating them well, responding to their needs. This was the philosophy of Harold's grandfather, running a horse drawn haulage business during Harold's childhood. Although the memories he shared of this were few, they are worth recounting. How, three days each week they took loads into Manchester, 12 miles each way. The other three days (working on the Sabbath being unheard of then – there was church or chapel to be seen at on Sundays in order to maintain a position of respectability in the community), the other three days were for local deliveries. Not to benefit the men, who walked the 12 miles to and from Manchester to avoid overloading the horses, but rather to ensure that the horses were rested sufficiently between their longer journeys. How old was Harold when he witnessed his grandfather terminating the employment of one of his drivers? We don't know but certainly old enough for this to be a significant lasting memory which he often shared with his children and later, in old age, with his grandchildren. Anyone who works with horses needs to be able, at times, to get a horse to back up, this is a very unnatural way for a horse to move, they are wary animals, they like to see where they're going, assess the dangers for themselves, make their own decisions about the safety of the movement. Left to themselves they do not move backwards but if a horse is to pull anything they have to be got between the shafts and that usually means backing them into position. It is this action that the memory Harold frequently recalled relates to. In the stable yard with his grandfather, both of them saw one of the drivers attempting to back a horse into the shafts. The driver didn't know they were there or he surely wouldn't have used the age old trick of kicking the horse knees, the shock and pain of this forcing the backwards move because horses, like people are easily manipulated through shock, pain or fear. Harold watched and learnt as his grandfather took the horse's bridle, either side of the head, and showed the man how to apply gentle pressure in order to back the horse slowly and safely into the shafts. Of course the man knew this, he worked with horses, but impatience, a desire for mastery, the need for an outlet for some anger or frustration of his own – we don't know what but he had allowed it to come between him and doing a good job and it cost him his job. Having shown him how the problem lay with himself and not with the horse Harold's grandfather calmly told him, 'get your cards, you're finished here'. Everyone who worked for your grandfather knew that all members of the team were to be respected, including the horses, and so they knew that such actions would not be tolerated by the man who refused to allow his drivers to carry whips. If they couldn't handle the horses without a whip they were no use to him.

Horses, after all are intelligent animals, just like people they can be bullied, intimidated, forced into unpleasant and dangerous situations but they remain intelligent. In the 14 months between the armistice to mark the supposed end of hostilities in what would become known as the First World War but was then known as the Great War and Harold's birth, horses requisitioned for the war returned to their homes. Many times Harold told the story of the horses from the local big estate. An estate with a pre-war stable of perhaps three or four dozen horses. Through the duration of this war about one million horses were requisitioned and sent to the battlefields in France. They were totally unsuited to this new age of warfare with its guns, canons and barbed wire, and with insufficient food and care to keep the living horses healthy. Only 6 percent of that one million returned home again. Almost all of the horses from this estate went to war, no more than half a dozen returned. On their return to their stable yard each was seen to walk straight to the stall they had occupied before their enforced departure to war. Despite the years of misery they had suffered they each remembered their own safe place.

Another, lighter, memory Harold shared, with the listener left to conjure in their own mind the amusing image the story portrayed. This story took place in Harold's childhood, still a time of small communities and big community involvement, still a time for Whitsun and Mayday parades. We don't know which the memory refers to or even Harold's age but those pieces of information are not important. Instead picture local businesses, most of whom used horses, taking this opportunity to advertise their trade. So here we have the local removal company. Horse drawn removal vans were very light in weight in comparison to their size. Loaded they were pulled by one or two strong horses but unloaded they weighed next to nothing. Here in this parade is the empty removal van, drawn by two tiny Shetland ponies, trotting along looking bewildered at each other, 'why does it take two of us to pull this?' because horses and ponies are intelligent they know that you don't work two for a job that only takes one. When the Shetland ponies heard the amusement of the watching people they probably thought the laughter was directed at the person who had thought the job would take two.

A Reduced Income

As a child and young man back in the early 1930's, in the days before the state welfare system was centralised and extended to take greater account of the needs of the people, Harold experienced the poverty of what was to become known as the great depression. In adulthood he saw the heyday of the welfare state. In old age he saw the demise of the welfare state and knowing, from the experiences of his childhood community, the effects cuts and austerity would have on the lives of families, the poverty, humiliation and despair those families would endure, the actions of the government in his final years distressed him greatly. The ways in which the government sought to move state welfare from a safety net to support people through life's crises and low points, to a means of subjugating the poor, the needy and the dispossessed, he knew reflected the fears that the dominating classes have. Is it a fear of revolution – or a fear that if the poor and needy are not kept poor and needy but given the means to flourish, then their places at the pit of society will be empty – waiting to be filled? Is it a fear that they, themselves might fill those spaces once the current poor and needy have the means to flourish, when their daily horror of not finding enough money to pay the gas bill and feed the children is lifted?

Back in the early 1930's families with a father in work, such as Harold's, kept going on a regular, albeit less adequate than needed, income. The massive physical labour needed, in those days before the rise of technology, to keep a household running usually meant that one income only was possible. The fortunes and futures of Harold's family were looking hopeful, a father earning money and, for Harold, at a time when most children started work at 14, because 'the state' still did not want the working classes educated beyond their usefulness to the dominating classes, for him a scholarship to grammar school. Who knows what paths his life might have taken but for the suicide of his father when Harold was 14. A suicide almost certainly resulting from the trauma of his enforced experiences in what was then triumphantly known as 'The Great War'.

Maybe Harold's mother seemed less sympathetic to his plight than he might have expected when he was summoned from a Latin class to the school headmaster's office to be told, by his mother, the news of his father's death. A mother now struggling to come to terms with not only the devastating news of the death of her husband but also the realisation that life would be very different from now on for herself and her two surviving children. Not least because of the necessity to now live a lie, to pretend her husband had slipped into the canal and drowned accidentally – after all this was the 1930's, an admission of suicide might alienate her and her children from their community – not a step to be taken lightly in those depression days when families relied on support from each other. Harold would later quote his mother's next words, after conveying the news of his father's death, as, 'you'll have to get a job now'. Of course we can't know if these were her actual words. But these were her words as interpreted by Harold as a 14 year old suddenly faced with the realisation that his father was gone. His dreams of education and a teaching career – a dream inspired by a History teacher skilled in bringing the past alive, keeping Harold eager to know more, were also gone. Did he ever see that teacher again? Did that teacher miss Harold's keen, enquiring mind and thirst for knowledge, in his class? Or was Harold no more than another unfortunate statistic in an era of unfortunate statistics? This we will never know.

And so a job was found for Harold, because that was the way of things when 14 year olds started work, the adults in their lives found them jobs. Even in that era of great depression jobs could be found for 14 year olds because the labour of a 14 year old came cheap. The job found for Harold, by who? His mother? A family friend? We don't know but we do know his job was with what was then known as the co-operative society, small general grocery stores that would, through Harold's lifetime evolve into one of the big supermarket chains, losing much of its attention to individual customers' requirements along the way. Like the way Harold's co-operative shop, the one where he had his first job, stocked chicken-in-aspic because one customer, and only one customer, wanted to buy it from time to time.

Of course, after some time working for the co-operative society Harold's true worth was recognised with a wage increase, or maybe he attained his 15th birthday, or possibly his 16th birthday, and so automatically qualified for a wage increase.

Whatever the reason for the increase it was fairly substantial at 25% bringing his weekly earnings from three shillings and four-pence to four shillings and three-pence. Did Harold experience a glow of excitement, of feeling appreciated, did he think how this would make life a little more comfortable for both himself and his family? Or, ultimately was there disappointment? Because this was the era when wages were handed over to mothers and spending money allocated. Harold's mother operated a straightforward system, she took the shillings and he kept the coppers. Before the pay rise she took three shillings and he kept four-pence, after the pay rise she took the four-shillings and Harold kept the three-pence – a 25% reduction!

Alcohol, Drugs and Wasted Lives

Growing up in those troubled times between what later become known as the two world wars, Harold must have witnessed a myriad of ways in which people got through their days. While cocaine reigned supreme at the dinner parties of many more moneyed communities during the 1930's, alongside expensive wines and spirits, as even today, the less moneyed members of society were not forgotten. Then there would be cheaper beer available to them during restricted licensing hours but now, thanks to social progress, cheap alcohol is available almost 24 hours a day. So far we have come!

The great thing about not drinking alcohol was that Harold was able to more easily observe its effects on others. Of course, most people have their own ideas of how drinking alcohol affects their behaviour but their assessment is already somewhat invalid by virtue of the fact that they have drunk alcohol and so are no longer functioning as themselves without alcohol. So many people think one drink makes no difference but you have only to watch them to observe those subtle differences emerging right from the first drink, almost from the first sip. Increasingly the evidence tells us that everything we put into, and do to, our bodies, makes a difference, what we eat, what we drink, what exercise we take, what substances we imbibe – prescribed, legal or otherwise. All these things influence what we become, both in the moment and in the longer term, they influence how we live, and often, how we die.

But what bothered Harold most about the effects of alcohol or drug use was the consequences for others of the consumer's actions. The distress caused to others, the damage to things that others valued resulting from the consumer making ill-informed decisions, taking ill-informed actions, doing harm to others. And the waste. The young man whose actions in the heat of an alcohol fuelled argument result in years imprisoned. And when he emerges from a prison yet more years spent trying against odds insurmountable by all but the most hardy and well-supported, to establish a place for himself in the community. Where did it go wrong for this young man? Harold would wonder because of one thing he was absolutely clear, no child is born bad. That was one of several things which puzzled him about the Church of England, with no original sin why the pressure for infant baptism?

And another thing of which Harold was absolutely clear, nobody should have to live without hope. Consequently he applauded the Norwegian system where nobody served more than a 17 year sentence. But here – a life sentence with a minimum term, parole hearings – will freedom come this year, next year, in 10 years, but even when it does come it's not real freedom because the prisoner is only on licence, easily recalled to prison at a moment's notice – not really a recipe for sound mental health, physical health, planning for a future, building a life, so maybe why bother! Lifers on parole, products of a justice system that is anything but just. A justice system wasting lives.

And a story of a crime averted by the actions of the intended victim, just instinctive actions taken on the spur of the moment. An elderly friend of Harold's, in his 80's, walking with a stick, threatened by three youths eager for whatever money or valuables he carried, each full of group courage and bravado and out to impress each other. But look! The elderly man has backed himself into a tight corner, only one of the youths will be able to approach him at a time, the elderly man raises his stick with both hands above head height, a very stout wooden walking stick it has all his strength behind it. He doesn't need his strength to support him, the wall behind him is doing that, 'Well', he says calmly, 'whose first', because if he's going down at least one of them is going with him, certainly with a split skull. And now all the group courage and bravado is gone, one will have to attack him first and they all know that one is getting a broken skull. None of them want to be that one, they back away, they're trying not to lose face so they shout a few insults while the elderly man ignores them. They all know who won.

A Time to be Born and a Time to Die

A certainty - For each of us there is a time when we are born and there is a time when we die. But these, our birth and our dying, our moving into this world and our leaving behind of this world have no pre-ordained time. Our birth is a game of chance, conceived this month we inherit these characteristics, conceived the following month we are a completely different person. Some of us will die old, some will die young, some will die when they are neither young nor yet old. Some will die at the hands of others, intentionally or through a failure to protect, while others will die by their own hand intentionally or through their own failure to protect and nurture themselves. We will all die when somebody still needs us.

Another certainty - we none of us pass through this world alone. We are not islands in a sea of humanity we are that sea, we are that humanity, even the most isolated or outcast persons live in a dependency on other people and the things that other people do.

There will be times when each of us may need to give something of ourselves to others, to friends, to family, to strangers, for no reason other than that they need our giving. For we none of us know when the time will come that we will need something of another person in order to make it through a moment, an hour, a day, a night. Then will that other person give what we need them to give? Or will they give only what they want to give? Will their giving be for us or will it be for them? Loudly made visible to the world 'look what I have done, look how kind, good and caring I am'. Or will they give quietly with the grace that can move mountains and leave the receiver better able to continue their struggle against the hand that life has dealt them?

We all, at some times in our lives, know the kindness of others, the goodness of others, and often we are surprised by who it is that is there to catch us as we fall and we may be equally surprised by who it is that stands back, almost gleefully, or maybe really gleefully, watching our fall. Harold's early experience of his father's death in adverse circumstances left him admirably positioned to know that after a death you find out who your true friends are, and you may be in for some surprises. The most valuable person to you at times of chaos and despair is not the one who sits drinking the tea you have made for them saying, 'now let me know if there's anything I can do', no that is not valuable because you won't let them know, you can't, all you can do is make it from one end of the day to the other. No, the most valuable person to you is the one that knocks on your door and says, 'I've come to take you for your food shopping' – or something similar, some basic everyday thing because at these times that is what you need. And patience, you need people to be patient. You need the patience of others because your brain and body are so completely taken up with that all important getting from one end of the day to the other that there is no space for deeper thoughts such as planning for tomorrow, or remembering what people have told you or what you have eaten or where you have been. When Harold cared for the father-in-law, with whom he had nothing in common and rarely saw, in the weeks after the death of his mother-in-law, he did so not just for himself, in fact not at all for himself, but for his wife who had lost her mother and for his father-in-law facing life without his wife after 57 years. Perhaps he did so because we can all respect another's suffering and hold them up a while, in the words of Harold's father-in-law at this time, 'You've shown me a lot of heart'. It never hurts to be kind.

Remember – our lives may be short or they may be long or they may be something in between short and long. Whichever it is there will come a day for each of us when to go back, to make amends, to apologise, to show someone we love them, to help that person when they needed us, will no longer be possible, for there is a time when we too shall die. There is no time to hate, no time to refrain from embracing, no time for war, but there is always time to care, time to be kind, and time to love.

Somewhere My Love

In every life, except perhaps for the very shortest of lives, there is loss. Loss of people, places or things we have loved, cherished or held dear. People leave us, places change, life takes unexpected turns with lasting consequences. We learn how to live with the decisions that we make, we learn how to live without the people, places and things that we have lost, often through a long despair akin to a long hard winter where snow covers the world we knew and seems as if it will never allow us the new beginning of Spring. And then our snow slowly melts away, leaving us to find those we have lost in a new place within us.

Aunty Mary off the Barges

Who was Mary? Well it's hard to know exactly, there being so very little that Harold knew about her Once she joined Harold's extended family she could only be the old Mary of her earlier years in her own memory, in her new life she had to be a new Mary and it seems that she may not have been so very skilled at being this new Mary. But possibly that's because nobody really wanted the new Mary in the family and they did their best to pretend she wasn't there, because she wasn't one of them.

Mary, we do know, was married to one of Harold's uncles. As a child and as a youth he observed her at the various gatherings that brought members of the extended family together, weddings, funerals, other celebrations or occasions for commiserations. But Mary was different, she didn't look different, no difference in colour, ethnicity, economic circumstances – they were all working class, meaning in the 1920's and 1930's, as it means today, not quite enough money to go round at best and a desperate need for more money at worst.

Either way, then or now, being working class meant reliance on others who were, themselves, more comfortably positioned. Maybe those responsible for deciding eligibility for government handouts, for deciding working hours, or for deciding how little you should expect to live on. People who never imagined themselves in the position of the working class, who still, to this day, deep down believe that there is a deserving poor and there are wasters, shirkers and undeserving poor, on whom they should not waste their time and charity. Charity giving, there's another thing that irked Harold. Not the giving to charity but the need for charity for things that really should be government funded, cancer research, heart disease research, and food banks! How have we come once again to this in a country that supposedly has the security of a welfare safety net to support the most vulnerable and those who need to get through the bad patch of a lost job, a death, or a health crises? How can a Universal 35 days wait for a first payment of universal credit help? Whose idea was that? Did they know that 35 days is just long enough to lose the fingertip grip with which many cling on?

But we digress and so back to Mary. Mary was from the barges, that much Harold knew because on different occasions members of the family would whisper this to the young Harold, making clear that Mary was not really one of this family even though she was married into it. Bargees' families were rough and ready, large families living in crowded conditions, for most of the barge had to be given over to the cargo, the transportation of which earned them a very meagre living.

Did Mary yearn for her earlier life? If little else life on the barges must have given a sense of freedom and a life lived at a horse's walking pace. No matter how urgent the delivery, how much the buyers and sellers of the goods might want them moved quickly, the barges still moved at the walking speed of a horse, a measured pace to ensure that the miles travelled each day were not onerous to the horse. After all no point in overworking the horse today for that would mean not being able to work the horse at all tomorrow. Slow and steady wins the race. In the end the factory owners, the coal mine owners, the business owners, all confident in their superior position in society, were and still are dependent on those who do for them the things they cannot or will not do for themselves. This is ever the case, no matter the money, position or prestige of a person we all depend on others.

Mary was tolerated at those family gatherings, possibly because Mary had the sense to keep quiet, blend into the background, not draw attention to herself, to pretend that she was not being ignored and whispered about, to know that, in the times in which she lived, this was where she was safest. A lifetime of being bottom of the heap, second rate, not quite a full family member, a lifetime's payback for flouting the expectations of the day and becoming pregnant before marriage.

Not much is said about this but these forced marriages surely also impacted on the men involved. We don't think that this was a case of love across boundaries, Harold's uncle falling unreservedly in love with Mary from the barges. Surely had that been the case he would not have tolerated the family's lack of respect for Mary when she became his wife, even if that was only shortly before the birth of their child. More likely that his liaison with Mary was an opportunity taken, expecting that Mary and her family would move on before any consequences were known. What then did he feel as he made his wedding vows to Mary, legally tied for a lifetime to a woman he had no feelings for, knowing how she would be looked on by his family? Did he and Mary, over the years, come to love and respect each other, or did they both live out their lives grieving for what might have been? We don't know. Harold's contact with them diminished as life took them in different directions and eventually they were gone, but not entirely, do we ever go entirely? For Mary lingered in Harold's memory at least into his own final year when he mentioned her again wondering how she had made peace with the life that came to her. For more than 90 years after knowing Mary he never dismissed her plight as just the way things were done then, he still questioned it and it influenced his belief that we should not be tied to such expectations. Some people would call Harold a maverick but really all he expected was that people should think for themselves, be themselves, and be proud of themselves, of others and of the choices that they make.

Blackberry Picking

The blackberries are gone now from the hedgerows where Harold used to take his children to pick them on late summer Saturdays, although they can still be found in abundance in other places. There were two favourite blackberrying places, both now changed, one almost beyond recognition, 'progress' as Harold would remark ironically.

Along the lane which ran behind the church yard of the small town Harold called home for the last 60 years of his long life. Into the fields at the end of the lane where the blackberries grew along the hedges that separated these fields from the grounds of what had once been the local big house, the Old Court. With the house lost in a fire before his arrival in the town the grounds would remain fenced, and increasingly wild, for many years before becoming a public amenity – well actually not all of the land became available to the public, large amounts of it were sold at a handsome profit for building. Of course, many young people of the town had always enjoyed the land, a way through a fence is not hard to find when there are rabbits, foxes and birds to be watched. Probably the more adventurous tried trapping the rabbits, maybe taking them home triumphantly as food, learning by instinct the survival skills of their predecessors. There were never any reports of anyone coming to harm, despite the large lake and the fact that many of these excursions took place in the hours of darkness. Perhaps, left to themselves, our young people are more able to look out for themselves and their friends than we give them credit for in our 21st century society.

Along that hedge the blackberries grew in abundance while the fields behind the backs of the pickers hummed with late summer life. At the top of those fields, a steep climb for very little legs, were big old horse chestnut trees to supply the schoolchildren with the conkers that would fill their time for a few weeks as they learnt about the merits of different sizes and shapes of conker and how to bake their conkers to harden them ready to do battle, at the end of a piece of string, with their opponents conkers. Woe betide the one who didn't tie the knot securely for their conker would surely fly away at the very first swing. Did the conker excitement of his children remind Harold of his youth? He never interfered, did he know that some things are best learnt by trial and error. There is surely more satisfaction to be gained by winning, or losing, with a conker prepared for battle by your own efforts, than winning or losing with a conker lovingly prepared for you by a parent. Which best prepares the child or youth for the challenges of life to come?

The blackberries are gone now from that hedge, the fields are gone also, given up for housing. Some of the conker trees remain at the top, causing a nuisance to the residents of those houses when they have the audacity to drop their harvest on the footpaths.

A plastic bag inside a paper bag – the perfect receptacle for blackberry picking, Harold must have invented that because there were no plastic bags in his youth, but what a perfect combination. The plastic keeping the blackberries secure, keeping leaking juice in, but plastic is slippery and easily lost from small, hot hands or hands sticky from the blackberries eaten along the way. The paper bag over the top to give form to this improvised harvesting receptacle, sitting securely in the palm of a hand or resting on the ground while those hard-to-reach blackberries were stretched for. Paper is, anyway, far more satisfying to hold than plastic, there's real sensory feedback from a paper bag. Small hands can scrunch down the top of a paper bag securing the harvest safe inside, but a plastic bag needs a knot at the top to keep its contents secure. The youngest children are not able to tie knots in plastic bags heavy with fruit. The paper bag over the plastic puts the child in control, it's one more thing they can do for themselves, an early experience of independence and responsibility – if they don't scrunch down the top of their bag securely the harvest could be lost, no blackberry and apple crumble for tea, no blackberry and apple jam through the winter, better to take the time to do the job well.

A second blackberry picking site, a longer walk, two fields to be crossed, sheep to be spotted although they always kept a safe distance, possibly disgruntled that people had come into their field to disturb their busy day of eating and resting and watching the world go by. Through the swing gate and onto the railway line, another victim of the Beeching cuts but the line still in place and, in the early days of Harold's life as a father in this town, still used by the occasional freight train. But, how fortunate, closing the railway line left a perfect place to put a by-pass in later years. That put an end to blackberry picking, the bushes still remain but what parent would pick blackberries at the side of the road with their children as traffic races by at 50 miles an hour? The progress of the modern age slowly eliminating the places where children played and learnt, and giving them sedentary pursuits as compensation – never mind that these would result in long term health problems, it's all in the name of progress. Even in those early days, before the by-pass, and the opening up of the Old Court land Harold knew that the lowest growing blackberries should be avoided in case these routes were used by dogs – although dog walking was not then the popular hobby it has become. Everyday life was still helping to keep people fit, they didn't have to depend on the demands of a pet to get them outside.

Harold never really understood the increasing mania for dog keeping – from his childhood he had learnt that dogs were for work, Chained outside the house with a kennel for shelter as they guarded the property and alerted the people within to potential danger, or given priority on the country buses as they travelled with the shepherd who worked alongside them. What disbelief he would express in later years at the money people would part with, and the lengths that they would go to, to keep dogs, pet dogs who do no work, alive. Pondering quietly how willingly would those same people spend that same money to protect their own health or that of their children? Indeed, even pondering how people are influenced to spend as much money destroying their own health as they spend in preserving the health of their dogs – a strange world indeed.

The Lost Child

Now here is something that Harold didn't talk about, at least not in terms of his own loss. Perhaps he felt that a mother's loss was greater and maybe he was right, or maybe not – we don't know for often when someone we love dies we each feel that our grief is the most powerful grief there is. We may struggle to know that the grief of another may surmount our own, to accept that sometimes we need to put our own grief aside for a while so that we may best support that other person as they slowly make their way through the depths of their grieving to reach a new and different life where the one they have lost is no longer a physical presence.

What we do know is that Harold lost, through stillbirth, a child that he must have hoped would live, and surely that caused him some sorrow. Did he initially hide his sorrow to support the greater loss of another person, his wife, mother of the dead child? And of his oldest child who, at the age of 5 or 6 was surely anticipating the arrival of a sibling eagerly? Or was he simply the product of an era when parents still expected that not all of their children would survive. He sometimes talked of his own two brothers, dead in infancy but we don't know why, probably he was never told the cause of death. In his youth infant death was commonplace and he himself, very young. But many times in later life he talked of seeing a baby brother swaddled after the fashion of the day, sleeping in a box or basket close to the fire – just for the few short weeks that such comfort was needed before death, when warmth and physical security are no longer necessary. The only certainty between birth and death is that time will pass, how much time each of us will have none of us can know, for Harold's brothers a few weeks for Harold 98 years and a few weeks.

Harold spoke of hearing the women in his childhood community sharing together the numbers of children they had lost through still-births and early deaths, for when something extraordinary happens people instinctively seek out others who have experienced the same or similar. These days they set up support groups and on-line communities to share their grief or joy where it will be best understood.   Later, in the 1950's, Harold's sister would lose her firstborn child, a daughter, and then Harold would lose a child, a son, did this seem more of an inevitability than a possibility? In the end the most enduring memorial to each one of us, no matter how short or long our lives, will surely be the memories carried in the hearts of those who have known and loved us, for whatever time there was. We all carry within us something of those who have gone before us and those we have lived alongside. This knowledge comforts us when we grieve for one whose physical presence is no more. And as Harold would have said if he were still here to read this – 'let's hope they carry the good bits'.

Memories for a Sister

Younger than Harold, after the death, in infancy, of his two brothers came Harold's sister. Was he close to his sister when they were children? Of course not many photographs were taken in those days but there is one, showing Harold and his sister sitting on a bench outdoors. Harold's feet just touching the ground while his sister's legs are not yet so long. She sits on her hands and swings her legs. She looks as if she is concentrating hard, trying to keep still long enough for the photograph to be taken, there is laughter in her eyes. Both children have an air of being happy and comfortable, was this a special occasion? Most likely it was for they are both very tidily dressed, hair neatly brushed or combed, this is not a spontaneous photo such as those that parents take continuously of their children in this, the 21st century, missing their children's childhood in a frenzied fear of not recording it sufficiently well, do they not know that childhoods are made of memories not photographs?

In those days, when Harold was perhaps ten years old, family photos were taken with a box brownie camera, eight exposures to a roll of film. For a working class family in the 1930's depression, developing the pictures would probably cost a small fortune, or at least a sizeable portion of the family funds for that week. So almost certainly this was a photograph taken to mark an occasion, was it Harold's occasion? His sister's occasion? Perhaps, if he were indeed 10 or 11 years old it was to mark his achieving a scholarship to grammar school. Or, just possibly, this was simply the last exposure on a film reel that needed developing quickly and his mother chose a moment, on a Sunday morning when they were clean and tidy ready for chapel, to photograph her two children together. Whatever the reason the photograph survived Harold's whole long life and beyond giving those that he left behind an enduring glimpse of his childhood. How could those two children know, when the photograph was taken, that their lives would soon be drastically changed by the death of their father and how could Harold or his sister know that her children's lives would be drastically changed forty years later when she also died too young?

Harold seldom talked much about his sister but sometimes she must have come to mind, probably much more than anyone ever knew. Occasionally his thoughts showed more openly with a comment when he briefly spotted a resemblance to his sister in one of his children, in looks or actions, in long hair tied back, 'I can see Molly in you like that'. In later years, when she was gone, in what ways did he remember her? When he lost touch with her children did it comfort him to find her again fleetingly in his own children?

During Harold's final days, when his physical presence in the world was gently fading, when his sight had faded far more than he ever wanted us to know, his words told us that his mind was busy with a lifetime of memories. A lifetime of 98 years holds a lot of memories. We had to piece together what he wanted us to know from the few words he shared with us in those final days. When he told us that, if we wanted to know more about the ancient Zoroastrian religion, we should look it up, he recalled that the information, in his childhood home, could be found in the corner of the living room in the blue book – was this somewhere he had sent his sister in earlier days to find things out for herself? 'Or the web', he said, 'you can use the web now'. Two different eras but from Harold the message remained the same right to his final day with us. Look things up, find things out, be interested and engage with the world, knowledge, education and skills won't come without effort, they need to be sought and valued. And always keep open a place in your thoughts for those who you have loved.

And finally

The world is more mystery than not, and we are ever in the presence of gifts beyond measure. In the quiet of our time, may we reach to touch that treasure and return to our lives with a new sense of kindness, care, and compassion for others. For kindness and love give our lives meaning and worth.

(Adapted from a Unitarian Prayer)